Love,
Toby

TOBY

LOST & FOUND

Written by Michele Terpin

Illustrated by Ron Wennekes

PAGE PUBLISHING, INC.
New York, NY

First originally published by Page Publishing, Inc. 2017

ISBN 978-1-64138-151-2 (Hardcover)
ISBN 978-1-64138-150-5 (Digital)

Printed in the United States of America

THANK YOU

Toby~Lost and Found is dedicated to the Michiana Humane Society of Michigan City, Indiana, and to all the wonderful organizations who find and care for lost and abandoned animals. Their aim is to find a "Forever Home" for all of them. I was very lucky to find **TOBY**.

To my Grandchildren, Hudson (Bear), Haddie, Harper, Olivia and Vivienne. I know they will have a great love and respect for all animals.

To Susan Block, my writing mentor and champion, who encouraged me to write *Toby~Lost and Found*. Susan passed away before this endeavor took shape. Thank you Susan.

For Nona who will always be my "Forever Home." We were so much more than friends. We were friends and family made in love and mutual respect, the best kind. You are always in my heart.

To Ken, my husband and partner of thirty years, I thank you. We share a love for nature and all its inhabitants. Our home has been blessed with love.

On a beautiful Fall day, I stopped by the Michiana Humane Society. I did not have a plan to bring home a dog or for that matter, look at any dogs. There was a cute blond girl at the front desk.

"I'm looking for a good natured, little lap dog," I said. "I cannot look at all of the dogs. I will feel bad and want to take them all home. But, if a dog comes in that fits my description, call me. I will give you my number."

As I started to recite the telephone number, the girl held up her hand and said, "I'll be right back."

This is how Toby's story begins.

I really love my yard. I love all the pretty flowers, trees and birds. But I want to see what the other side of this fence looks like. I want to explore.

Look, the gate is open. Now is my chance. Hello world, here I come!

Where am I? I ran and ran past the trees and cows. I even crossed the road... things I never saw before. It was very noisy outside of my yard.

I'm afraid. I'm tired.
I need to lie down.

5

Oh no! Who is this? Somebody is coming. He is big and yellow with a funny hat. He's coming to pick me up. I hope he is nice. I am not supposed to go with a stranger, but I'm lost.

I'm so tired. I can't run.
Maybe he is taking me home. I
really want my bed.

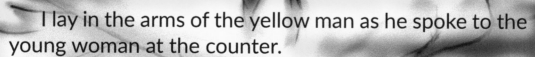

I lay in the arms of the yellow man as he spoke to the young woman at the counter.

"I found him in the grass by Jenkins Farm," he said. "He is really dirty and wet. He doesn't have a collar but seems friendly and very tired."

The nice young woman at the desk thanked him. "He must be lost. We'll take good care of him."

Because I was so dirty, the young lady gave me two baths. She then gave me something to eat, not my regular food. It was OK. I am so tired. I am confused and a little scared.

When I woke up there were lots of other dogs in crates like the one I'm in. There are little dogs and big dogs, loud barks and not so loud barks.

A little dog like me was crying. Was she lost too? Maybe I'll talk to her. But then I miss my home too much to talk. I will never run away again. I was happy at my home.

There was a big dog with black dots all over.

"Hey, here is the new kid," the Dalmatian said.

A funny floppy eared dog, the Cocker Spaniel said, "You're cute! I think your name is Toby. I heard the ladies call you that."

I don't think that's my name. As long as they don't call me Dopey, I guess it's OK. Toby, T O B Y, sounds good.

April is such a kind person. All the dogs love her because she carries treats for us in her pocket. She picks me up. Maybe she's taking me for a walk. No walk today. She carried me through the big doors. I see a lady waiting. She looks nice. She's smiling at me?

I look at her too. Is she going to bring me home? Is she going to be my new Mom?

April said, "We call him Toby. The name just fits him."

The nice lady said I was just perfect! "I will take very good care of him and keep his name TOBY."

We're going somewhere. I hope it's some place nice. I like this beautiful car. "I love you!" said Mom.

After we get settled in my new home, Mom said we will start training. My training is to help me be a good dog. I will be a Companion Dog. That means I will go everywhere with Mom. I am a very special dog. I will learn to be the best I can be. I will stay by my Mom's side and be the best company for her.

We went to see Dr. Mac at the Veterinary Hospital. I got a rabies shot and shots to prevent me from getting bad things. He looked me over from nose to tail. He said I was in, "good shape." I have to go back to have my teeth cleaned. I was not good at brushing my teeth. Mom will brush them for me.

I'm ready to go home.

We are celebrating Thanksgiving. I don't
know what that means, but everyone is saying
"Happy Thanksgiving." Holidays are very nice.
We eat special food with good friends.

My new friends are Maggie and Molly. I will always remember my first holiday with my new family.

Our exercise after a big meal is running. Three happy dogs, running and jumping all over Honey Hill Farm. My friends the Spaniels, Maggie and Molly, love to play. I am much smaller than they are.

Sometimes they run so fast that they run over me and I tumble down the hill. We play all day until it is time for dinner. Turkey again.

I have such a good time running! Mom takes me to the golf course. I run up and down, round and round. Oh boy, sometimes I see squirrels. I even see deer. Mom tells me to watch quietly as big men are hitting a little white ball. I know Maggie and Molly would love to play here too. When they come to visit, we will go to the golf course.

Yes, today it is time for lessons. I am excited because we go to a big barn to learn. There are big dogs and little dogs. I listen and am mostly quiet. I want to earn my beautiful badge. Mom told me I will get a Companion Badge, when I pass all my tests.

To be a Companion Dog means I have passed all my training. I am able to go everywhere, travel and shop with Mom. I will be the best company for her. I will sit on Mom's lap and be by her side to let her know I am her best friend.

Here we go. First I need to learn to sit quietly. I learn to bow my head to the floor. "Down," means to lie down. "Heel," means to sit by my Mom's side at attention. When I do these right, I get a treat. I like being right and getting treats.

I am working so hard. I learn to listen, to not bark and to come when I am called. I can pick up my leash and my toys. I am so happy! I get so many hugs, kisses and treats. Mom tells me I am a GOOD BOY!

I hope to get a beautiful Companion Badge. Then everyone will know I am special. I am a Companion Dog with a new home. I will never be lost again.

My Mom takes me everywhere. She tells me I am the best dog ever and how lucky she is to have me. We sit together and take drives together. She always hugs me and tells me she loves me. I know I am loved. I was a lost and unhappy dog. She found me and now I have the best Mom.

I am happy right where I am and will never leave home again.